# AFTER THE FEAST
## A Turkey Leftovers Cookbooklet

Iva Cheung

NEW WESTMINSTER

Text and janky illustrations copyright © 2025 by Iva Cheung

ISBN 978-1-7782897-5-0 (PDF)
ISBN 978-1-7782897-7-4 (hardcover)
ISBN 978-1-7782897-6-7 (paperback)

Hastily Assembled Books
(Iva Cheung's hastily assembled self-publishing outfit)
New Westminster, British Columbia
ivacheung.com

Proofreading by Grace Yaginuma
Cover illustration by Iva Cheung, using a reference image from freefoodphotos.com
Design by Iva Cheung
Printed and bound by IngramSpark

**Unless otherwise specified**
- Salt is kosher
- Pepper is freshly ground black
- Eggs are large
- Cucumbers are long English
- Oven is conventional—decrease temperature by 25°F (14°C) if using a convection oven

**Two dollars from each print copy sold support food security initiatives in Nunavut through the Qajuqturvik Community Food Centre (qajuqturvik.ca).**

# Contents

iv   Introduction

## Getting the most out of your bird

- 2   Turkey stock
- 4   Bonus: Vegetable crackers
- 6   Turkey schmalz
- 6   Crispy turkey skin

## Using your leftovers

- 10   Breakfast hash
- 12   Turkey cranberry sandwich
- 13   Bonus: Ideas for leftover cranberry sauce
- 14   Turkey bánh mì
- 16   Turkey pie
- 18   Turkey cottage pie
- 20   Turkey wild rice soup
- 22   Turkey & corn egg-drop soup
- 24   Turkey corn chowder
- 26   Turkey tom kha
- 28   Turkey, sweet potato & peanut stew
- 30   Turkey quesadillas
- 32   Sheet-pan turkey fajitas
- 34   Turkey enchiladas
- 36   Turkey salad with cranberries & pecans
- 38   Turkey cellophane noodle salad
- 40   Turkey laab
- 42   Gochujang cashew turkey
- 44   Saag turkey
- 46   Turkey curry rice
- 48   Hainanese turkey rice
- 50   Turkey fried rice
- 52   Turkey okonomiyaki
- 54   Turkey kookoo
- 56   Turkey croquettes

58   Index

# Introduction

Have you cooked a turkey for your holiday get-together and now you're stuck with an obscene amount of leftover turkey meat you're wondering how to use up?

Over the years I've experimented with ways to use turkey leftovers, and I've collected some of my favourites here. I'm grateful to draw from a variety of culinary traditions, but I make no claim to authenticity. My goal is simply to share tasty, nourishing recipes using ingredients that are easy to find for a home cook like me.

I also assume that because you've probably already spent a full day preparing a turkey-centric feast, you'd want your leftover turkey meals to be easy, so although a handful of these recipes are a bit more involved, most are pretty straightforward. These recipes are meant to spark ideas, so don't feel wedded to the specific ingredients or techniques, and feel free to use whatever you have on hand.

Turkey is famously bland and dry, but I see that as a feature, not a bug—an opportunity to add virtually any flavour you want. You'll notice that a lot of the recipes involve marrying the turkey meat with a seemingly gratuitous amount of sauce. That said, turkey does have its own aroma and taste (the smell of a roasting turkey is unmistakable and nostalgic for a lot of us), and rather than just adapting chicken recipes, I've suggested some ways to bring out and highlight turkey's turkeyness in these dishes.

Because different turkeys prepared in different ways—wet brined, dry brined, brine-injected, unbrined, etc.—can have varying amounts of salt, as can leftover sides like mashed potatoes that appear in some of these dishes, **I've erred on the side of under-seasoning in these recipes, with the intent that you'll taste and adjust salt levels to your preference.**

Where I was directly inspired by an existing recipe, I've credited the authors and added a link. (Those of you reading a print copy can find URLs after the index.) The originators of many of the dishes in this book, though, have been lost to time. I'd copied the recipes onto index cards and tweaked them over iterations.

I hope these recipes help you celebrate your leftovers instead of getting sick of them!

# Getting the most out of your bird

# Turkey stock

I might enjoy turkey soup more than the turkey itself. Don't throw out that carcass! Take off any skin to make crispy turkey skin (page 6), then simmer the rest of the carcass with vegetables to get a flavourful stock. I like to add a splash of acid to draw out more of the minerals from the bones, and after simmering, I pick the carcass clean. There can be several cups of meat left on those bones that you can use in soups and other dishes, including turkey laab (page 40).

**Yield: ??? Depends on the size of your carcass. I usually get at least 3 qt (3 L).**

1 turkey carcass
1 onion, quartered
2 carrots, cut into 2-inch (5-cm) chunks
2 ribs celery, cut into 2-inch (5-cm) chunks
3 cloves garlic, gently smashed
1 tsp (5 mL) black peppercorns
2 sprigs fresh thyme (or ½ tsp/2.5 mL dried thyme leaves)
1 sprig fresh rosemary (or 1 tsp/5 mL dried rosemary leaves)
1 bay leaf (Feel free to omit unless you've got fresh or frozen ones. I'm almost positive dried supermarket bay leaves don't do anything.)
2 Tbsp (30 mL) white wine or vinegar (apple cider or white wine work)

Put all the ingredients in a stockpot or pressure cooker and add enough water to cover by about 1 inch (2 cm).

If using a stockpot, bring to a boil on high heat, then turn the heat to low and simmer for 3–4 hours, topping up the water so that it covers the carcass. If using a pressure cooker, set it to pressure cook on high for 45 minutes, then allow it to release the pressure naturally.

Strain the stock through a sieve or colander into another pot—oh my god, don't absentmindedly pour it down the sink—and portion it out into smaller containers to cool quickly, then store in the fridge for up to 4 days or in the freezer indefinitely. (I don't think I'm technically supposed to imply that something is food-safe in the freezer indefinitely, but for our purposes, I think it basically is?)

When the turkey carcass is cool, pick any remaining meat off the bones and store it in the fridge or freezer for later use. I find it helpful to portion it out into 1-cup (250-mL) deli containers.

# BONUS: Vegetable crackers

Some more-ambitious-than-me people turn the vegetables from the stock-making process into crackers. Even my pathologically frugal ass is usually content to just compost the scraps, but in the spirit of reducing waste, I tried making crackers with the recipe below, adapted from [MJ & Hungryman](), and it does produce tasty results (the cheese does a lot of heavy lifting).

But are these crackers worth the faff? ~Enh~.

Vegetable scraps from making turkey stock (page 2)
1½ cups (375 mL) flour, plus more as needed
½ tsp (2.5 mL) baking powder
½ tsp (2.5 mL) salt
3 Tbsp (45 mL) olive oil or melted butter
½ tsp (2.5 mL) garlic powder
½ tsp (2.5 mL) chopped fresh rosemary or sage
¼ tsp (1.2 mL) pepper
¼ cup (60 mL) finely grated cheese (parmesan, pecorino, cheddar, and Gruyère all work well)

Rescue whatever vegetable scraps you want for your crackers—I tend to use only the softened veggies and discard the more fibrous scraps, like onion and garlic skins, thyme and rosemary stems, and bay leaves—and purée them with an immersion blender or in a food processor. The mixture will be quite wet. Transfer the mixture to a fine-mesh sieve to drain for 1–2 hours. You should end up with 1 cup (250 mL), give or take, of vegetable mush.

In a large mixing bowl, combine flour with baking powder, salt, olive oil or melted butter, garlic powder, rosemary or sage, pepper, cheese, and the drained vegetable purée. Stir until you have a shaggy dough. If the dough is too wet, add flour 1 Tbsp (15 mL) at a time until it's no longer sticky. Cover and chill in the fridge for at least 1 hour.

Preheat the oven to 350°F (180°C).

Divide the dough in half, and roll each half out to a $1/16$-inch (1.5-mm) thickness between two sheets of parchment. Remove the top sheet of parchment and cut the dough in a grid to delineate individual crackers. Transfer each sheet of parchment with the dough onto a sheet pan and bake for 15 minutes. Flip the crackers and bake for another 10 minutes or until the crackers turn golden-brown and reach your preferred level of crunch.

# Turkey schmalz

Schmalz is the fat that renders out of the bird as it cooks, mostly from the skin. At our Christmas dinners my in-laws used to jar it up and throw it out, but one year I offered to take it home if they weren't going to use it, and I've been the beneficiary of their Christmas turkey schmalz ever since.

Turkey schmalz works great as a cooking oil, and I even use it to make pastry (see page 16). It's an essential part of why turkey smells and tastes like turkey.

**Yield: ??? Depends on how big the turkey is and how fatty its skin is. I expect about 2 cups (500 mL) from a 15- to 20-lb (7- to 9-kg) turkey.**

Skim the layer of fat that rises from the drippings of a roasted turkey and put it in a jar in the fridge, where it will solidify (though not particularly hard). Use it in place of other cooking oil whenever you want to infuse your dish with the essence of turkey.

If you're not using it soon, you could remelt the schmalz and pass it through a coffee filter or paper towel to strain out the solid bits, which could make the fat go rancid more quickly if left in. I usually go through my schmalz pretty quickly, though, so I don't bother.

Make crispy turkey skin (below) to get even more schmalz.

# Crispy turkey skin

Roasted turkey skin goes from crispy to flabby disappointingly quickly, but it's easy to crisp back up—and in the process extract more schmalz to add to your collection. After you separate the skin from the meat and render out the remaining fat, it tends to stay crispy for a few days if you store it in the fridge in an airtight container. I like to crumble crispy turkey skin onto salads or soups or, if I'm being honest, I often just eat it like potato chips.

**Yield: ??? Depends on how much of the turkey skin you've already eaten.**

Pull off whatever remaining turkey skin you have and put it onto a rimmed sheet pan. Bake it at 275°F (135°C) (no need to preheat) for about 30 minutes and check if the fat has rendered out and the skin is crispy. If so, you're done. If not, continue baking, checking every 5 minutes.

Move the crispy skin onto paper towels to drain. Using a silicone spatula, scrape the rendered fat from the sheet pan into a jar and store it in the fridge. If not using the skin right away, store in an airtight container in the fridge for up to 4 days.

# Using your leftovers

# The obvious: Feast 2.0

There's nothing wrong with having a repeat of your turkey dinner the day after your turkey dinner. It's easy! The food's all there! What's not to love?

# Breakfast hash

Leftover vegetables like Brussels sprouts, carrots, or green beans work well in this recipe. Just cut them to the same size as your potatoes and stir them in along with the turkey. You could fry your eggs separately if you prefer having more control over their texture, but the method below involves cooking the eggs in situ for simplicity. Leftover cranberry sauce pairs beautifully with this dish.

**Yield: 4 servings**

1 lb (450 g) potatoes or sweet potatoes, cut into ½-inch (1-cm) cubes
3 cups (750 mL) diced raw or cooked hardy vegetables, like bell peppers, broccoli, carrots, green beans, Brussels sprouts, rutabaga, or beets
3 Tbsp (45 mL) turkey schmalz or other cooking oil, divided
1 onion, diced
1 clove garlic, minced
1 jalapeño, small diced
10½ oz (300 g) cooked turkey, cut into ½-inch (1-cm) cubes (about 2 cups/500 mL)
1 tsp (5 mL) ground cumin
1 tsp (5 mL) smoked paprika
½ tsp (2.5 mL) dried oregano
Salt and pepper to taste

Parcook the potato: Place the cubes in a microwave-safe dish, add 2 Tbsp (30 mL) water, then cover the dish with a lid or plate. Microwave on high for 3 minutes. Drain and set aside to cool slightly.

If your diced vegetables are raw, you can parcook them in the same way: Place them in a microwave-safe dish with 2 Tbsp (30 mL) water, then cover and microwave on high for 3 minutes. Drain and set aside to cool.

Preheat the oven to 350°F (180°C). (Or, if you'd rather not use the oven and do everything on the stovetop, see below.)

In a large oven-safe skillet, heat 2 Tbsp (30 mL) schmalz or oil on medium-high. Add the potato cubes and cook for 3 minutes to crisp up one side of the cubes. Stir and cook for another 3 minutes to crisp up another side of the cubes. Stir again and cook for another 3 minutes. Add onion, garlic, and jalapeño and cook for 3–5 minutes until the onion is soft and the garlic is fragrant.

Add the diced vegetables and stir for 1 minute until they're heated through. If you used hardier raw vegetables like carrots and beets, you might have to cook them for a bit longer until they're tender to your liking.

Add turkey, cumin, smoked paprika, oregano, salt, and pepper. Stir until well mixed, and adjust seasoning to taste.

4 eggs
½ cup (125 mL) shredded cheddar or other melty cheese
1 green onion, sliced
Crispy turkey skin, crumbled

Make 4 divots in the hash. Divide the remaining 1 Tbsp (15 mL) schmalz or oil among these divots, then crack an egg into each one. Fry for 1 minute, then transfer the skillet to the oven and bake for 5 minutes. Sprinkle everything with cheese, then continue baking until the eggs are done to your liking, 2–5 minutes. (Alternatively, you could avoid the oven altogether and finish the eggs on the stovetop, but in my experience this means either waiting a long time—because the hash acts a bit like an insulator, keeping the eggs from cooking quickly—or covering the skillet to trap in the heat and losing some of the crisp of the potatoes.)

Garnish with green onions and crumbled turkey skin and serve.

# Turkey cranberry sandwich

A classic use for turkey leftovers, so I couldn't not include it! I like to add peppery greens like arugula or mizuna, but you can use lettuce, spinach, or any other salad green you like.

**Yield: 1 sandwich**

- 1 Tbsp (15 mL) honey mustard (or mix 1 tsp/5 mL honey with 2 tsp/10 mL Dijon mustard)
- 2 slices bread of your choice
- 1¾ oz (50 g) brie, sliced
- 2½ oz (70 g) cooked turkey, sliced
- 2 Tbsp (30 mL) cranberry sauce
- 1 handful (about ⅓ oz/10 g) arugula or mizuna
- A few slices (about ⅓ oz/10 g) red onion

Spread ½ Tbsp (7.5 mL) honey mustard on one side of each slice of bread. On one slice, layer the brie, turkey, cranberry sauce, arugula or mizuna, and onions. Top with the second slice of bread, mustard-side down. (Did I really just spell out how to assemble a sandwich? I guess this section would have looked empty without instructions.)

# BONUS: Ideas for leftover cranberry sauce

These suggestions are for cranberry sauce made from fresh or frozen whole cranberries. I don't have experience with the jelly variety, so I can't really speck to how to use that up, although some of these ideas would probably still work. Where I live, cranberries come in 12-oz (340-g) bags, making 2 cups (500 mL) of sauce, and I always end up with extra of this chunky, tart condiment that sits somewhere between a jam and a compote.

1. **Stir it into yogurt**—Combine 2 Tbsp (30 mL) of cranberry sauce with ½ cup (125 mL) Greek yogurt, then add a handful of nuts and seeds. (Add granola if you'd like!) Spice it up with cinnamon and cardamom and sweeten it to taste with honey or maple syrup.

2. **Make it into chutney**—In a small saucepan, combine ¼ cup (60 mL) diced dried fruit (like dried apricot, dried pineapple, or candied ginger), a diced apple or pear, ¼ cup (60 mL) orange juice, 3 Tbsp (45 mL) brown sugar, 2 Tbsp (30 mL) apple cider vinegar, the zest of ½ orange, and a pinch each of cinnamon, ground cloves, ground cardamom, ground ginger, and chili flakes. Bring to a boil, and then simmer 8–10 minutes till the dried fruit has rehydrated and the apple or pear has softened. Stir in the cranberry sauce, then (carefully—it's hot!) taste and adjust sweetness or acidity to your liking with brown sugar and vinegar. Bring the mixture to at least 160°F (72°C), then transfer it to a sterilized, heatproof jar. Carefully cover with the lid and let it cool completely before refrigerating. Enjoy this chutney with cheese, roasted meats, grilled hardy vegetables, or Indian curries and flatbreads.

3. **Use it as a cheesecake topping**—Use whatever store-bought or homemade cheesecake you'd like, but here's an easy recipe for cheesecake cupcakes: Add paper liners to 10 cupcake tins (standard 2¾-inch/7-cm diameter), then beat together 8 oz (250 g) cream cheese with 2 tsp (10 mL) orange juice, 2 eggs, ⅓ cup (80 mL) granulated sugar, and the zest of ½ orange until smooth. Place 1 vanilla wafer (like Nilla) in each cupcake liner, then distribute the cheesecake batter among the lined tins. Bake at 300°F (150°C) for 20 minutes or until just set. Let them cool completely (and refrigerate if not using them right away). Top each cheesecake with 1 Tbsp (15 mL) cranberry sauce and serve!

# Turkey bánh mì

Your choice of bread—not the fillings—will determine how much you like this recipe. Vietnamese baguettes, unsurprisingly, work best because they've got a satisfying crisp exterior while also yielding to the bite, whereas some "artisanal" French-style baguettes will *obliterate* the roof of your mouth. Recipes that ambiguously call for "baguette" can send unsuspecting folks down a path of palate-demolishing pain and unfair assessments of bánh mì. If you can't get your hands on Vietnamese baguette, choose an airy, soft bread meant for sandwiches like a hoagie roll or even a kaiser roll. In this case I think texture is more important than shape.

You can make the pickled vegetables arbitrarily far in advance. Don't have daikon? Red radish, black radish, salad turnips, and even green cabbage all work as substitutes.

**Yield: 1 sandwich**

### Pickled vegetables

¼ cup (60 mL) julienned carrots (about 2¼ oz/65 g)
¼ cup (60 mL) peeled and julienned daikon radish (about 2¼ oz/65 g)
¼ cup (60 mL) sliced onion (about 1½ oz/40 g)
½ cup (125 mL) rice vinegar (white wine vinegar, apple cider vinegar, or white distilled vinegar all work)
¼ cup (60 mL) granulated sugar
¼ cup (60 mL) water

### Pickled vegetables

Place carrots, daikon, and onion in a heatproof jar.

In a small pot, combine vinegar, sugar, and water and bring to a boil, stirring to ensure all the sugar has dissolved. Pour the liquid over the vegetables in the jar and allow to cool completely. Store in the fridge until ready to use. ☞☞☞

## Turkey bánh mì

3½ oz (100 g) cooked turkey, sliced
1 Tbsp (15 mL) hoisin sauce
Pinch of pepper
12-inch (30-cm) Vietnamese baguette
3 Tbsp (45 mL) mayo (I use Kewpie)
1¾ oz (50 g) cucumber, thinly sliced
6–8 sprigs of cilantro
1 jalapeño, thinly sliced (optional)
1 wedge lime

## Turkey bánh mì

In a small bowl, toss together turkey, hoisin sauce, and pepper until the turkey is evenly coated.

Cut the bread in half to separate its top from its bottom. Spread mayo over both cut surfaces. On the bottom half, layer on the turkey, cucumber, pickled vegetables, cilantro (pick off the leaves and just use those if you don't like the stems), and jalapeño (if using), then squeeze some lime juice overtop before topping the sandwich.

Cut the sandwich in half crosswise (on a bias if you feel ~fancy~) and enjoy.

# Turkey pie

I find pie dough made with turkey schmalz crumblier than a traditional all-butter pie dough, so you might have to press it into a pie plate rather than rolling it out and draping it in, although using parchment does help. I use a mix of schmalz and butter for best results. My home-rendered fats also tend to have a higher water content than store-bought fats, so I typically don't have to add liquid to this pie dough to get it to hang together. I'm ambiguous about the type of flour to use because I've made it with all-purpose, whole wheat, whole-grain spelt, and Bob's Red Mill's 1-to-1 gluten-free flour, and although they all produce different results, they all work.

The pie filling is a great way to use other turkey feast leftovers, like carrots or green beans. If you do use already cooked vegetables, dice and stir them into the filling at the end of the stovetop cooking phase.

**Yield: 6-8 servings**

### Turkey schmalz pie dough

2½ cups (625 mL) flour
½ tsp (2.5 mL) salt
4 oz (112 g) butter, diced then chilled
4 oz (112 g) turkey schmalz, chilled
Ice-cold water, if needed

### Pie filling

2 Tbsp (30 mL) turkey schmalz or other cooking oil
1 onion, diced, or 1 leek, thoroughly rinsed and sliced
1 carrot, diced
1 rib celery, diced
1 clove garlic, minced
2 sprigs fresh thyme (or ½ tsp/2.5 mL dried thyme leaves)

### Turkey schmalz pie dough

In a large mixing bowl, combine flour and salt. Add butter and schmalz, and, using a pastry cutter, fork, or table knife, cut the fat into the flour mixture until well combined. The fat might have enough moisture that the dough comes together without added water, but if your mixture is too dry to stick together, add ice water 1 Tbsp (15 mL) at a time until the dough just comes together. It can take some time for the flour to hydrate, so start with a bit less water than you think you need, and it might cohere after a few minutes. Cover the dough and chill it in the fridge for at least 30 minutes.

### Pie filling

Heat schmalz or oil in large skillet on medium-high, then add onion or leek, carrot, and celery. Sauté until the onion or leek is soft and translucent, 2–3 minutes. Add garlic, thyme, rosemary, and sage and cook until fragrant, about 1 minute. Stir in the flour, then slowly add the stock, stirring constantly to prevent lumps. Add milk, cream, potatoes, rutabaga (if using), and salt. Bring to a boil,

### Pie filling *(cont'd)*

- 1 tsp (5 mL) chopped fresh rosemary (or ½ tsp/2.5 mL dried rosemary)
- 1 tsp (5 mL) chopped fresh sage (or ½ tsp/2.5 mL dried sage)
- ¼ cup (60 mL) all-purpose flour
- 1 cup (250 mL) turkey or other stock
- 1 cup (250 mL) whole milk
- 1 cup (250 mL) whipping cream
- 1 potato, peeled and diced (about 5¼ oz/150 g)
- 5¼ oz (150 g) rutabaga, diced (optional)
- ¾ tsp (4 mL) salt
- ½ cup (125 mL) green beans or snap peas cut into 1-inch (2-cm) segments (or frozen peas)
- 10½ oz (300 g) cooked turkey, cut into ½-inch (1-cm) cubes (about 2 cups/500 mL)
- ¾ cup (180 mL) corn (about ½ of an 12-oz/341-mL can)
- Salt and pepper to taste

### Assembly

- 1 egg, beaten with 1 Tbsp (15 mL) water or milk

then reduce the heat to medium and simmer until the potatoes and rutabaga are tender and the sauce is thick, about 15–20 minutes.

If you used thyme sprigs, fish out and discard the stems. Add green beans or snap peas, turkey, and corn and allow them to heat through, 1–2 minutes. Remove from the heat. The beans might be on the raw side now, but they will continue cooking as the pie bakes. Taste and adjust seasoning with salt and pepper.

### Assembly

Preheat the oven to 425°F (220°C).

Divide your pie dough in half and roll each half out between 2 sheets of parchment until the sheet of dough is big enough to cover the bottom and sides of a 9-inch (23-cm) pie plate (1 inch/2 cm deep), with about ½ inch (1 cm) of overhang on the edges. Drape the dough into the pie plate, working it into the corner where the bottom meets the sides.

Transfer the filling into the bottom crust.

Roll out the other half of the crust and drape it on top of the filling, sealing the edges with a fork or your fingers. Brush the top crust with egg wash, then, using a paring knife, jab a few slits in the top crust to allow steam to escape. (If you have extra egg wash that you don't want to waste, throw it into an okonomiyaki—see page 52.)

Put the pie plate on a sheet pan to catch any drips and bake for 35–40 minutes or until the crust is golden brown. Allow the pie to sit for about 10 minutes before cutting into it.

# Turkey cottage pie

This recipe can accommodate more than just leftover mashed potatoes. Cooked hardy vegetables like Brussels sprouts, carrots, or green beans can be diced and stirred into the filling at the end of the stovetop phase. Mashed vegetables like sweet potato or rutabaga can be added to the topping. If you have leftover gravy, you can use that instead of adding flour and stock.

Miso paste obviously isn't traditional (so skip it if you don't have any on hand), but I've found it a reliable way to bump up the umami that turkey tends to lack compared with the more conventional ground lamb or beef. Be sure to taste the filling before adding any more salt, though!

**Yield: 4 servings**

2 Tbsp (30 mL) turkey schmalz or other cooking oil
1 onion, finely diced
1 carrot, finely diced
1 rib celery, finely diced
½ cup (125 mL) green beans or snap peas cut into ½-inch (1-cm) segments (or frozen peas)
½ Tbsp (7.5 mL) miso paste
1 cup (250 mL) turkey or other stock
1 clove garlic, minced
¼ tsp (1.2 mL) chili flakes
2 sprigs fresh thyme (or ½ tsp/2.5 mL dried thyme leaves)
1 tsp (5 mL) chopped fresh rosemary (or ½ tsp/2.5 mL dried rosemary)
1 Tbsp (15 mL) tomato paste
2 Tbsp (30 mL) all-purpose flour

In a 10-inch (25-cm) oven-safe skillet, heat schmalz or oil on medium-high. Add onion, carrot, celery, and green beans or snap peas and sauté until the vegetables have softened, 3–4 minutes.

Meanwhile, in a medium bowl or liquid measuring cup, stir or whisk the miso paste into the stock until it's evenly distributed and set this mixture aside.

To the skillet, add garlic, chili flakes, thyme, and rosemary, and cook until garlic is fragrant, about 1 minute. Add tomato paste, and cook for another 30 seconds. Add flour and stir to distribute, then pour in the miso-stock mixture, stirring to work out any lumps of flour. Bring to a boil and cook until the sauce has thickened into a gravy consistency. Stir in Worcestershire sauce, turkey, and corn and allow these to heat through, about 1 minute, before removing the skillet from the heat. Carefully taste this turkey filling and season to taste with salt and pepper. If you used fresh thyme sprigs, fish out and discard the stems.

- 1 Tbsp (15 mL) Worcestershire sauce
- 10½ oz (300 g) cooked turkey, cut into ½-inch (1-cm) cubes (about 2 cups/500 mL)
- ¾ cup (180 mL) corn (about ½ of a 12-oz/341-mL can)
- Salt and pepper to taste
- 2 cups (500 mL) leftover mashed potatoes or 1 lb (450 g) potatoes, boiled until soft and mashed with 2 Tbsp (30 mL) butter, 2 Tbsp (30 mL) Greek yogurt, and ½ tsp (2.5 mL) salt (or to taste) and ¼ tsp (1.2 mL) pepper (or to taste)
- ½ cup (125 mL) shredded cheddar cheese, divided
- ¼ cup (60 mL) freshly grated parmesan cheese

Preheat the oven to 350°F (180°C).

Mix mashed potatoes with half of the cheddar. Spread this potato mixture over the turkey filling in the skillet. Top with the remaining cheddar and the parmesan. Bake 30–35 minutes until the cheese topping starts turning golden brown. Rest for 10 minutes before serving.

# Turkey wild rice soup

A classic for a reason! The smell of simmering turkey soup is like a warm hug. If you don't have wild rice (understandable, because it can be $$$), brown rice or barley work well, too. Orzo, short pasta like elbow macaroni, and white rice are also excellent carby options, but they'll need less time to simmer, so add them only for the last 8–10 minutes of cooking. If you have leftover gravy that you don't have other plans for, add it to this soup! Because gravy is essentially thickened stock, it'll blend seamlessly into the soup while its starches add body to the broth. And the herbs that typically go into gravy pair well with this soup's flavour profile.

**Yield: 4–6 servings**

2 Tbsp (30 mL) turkey schmalz or other cooking oil
1 onion, diced
2 carrots, diced
2 ribs celery, diced
2 sprigs fresh thyme (or ½ tsp/2.5 mL dried thyme leaves)
4 cups (1 L) turkey or other stock
2 cups (500 mL) water
10½ oz (300 g) cooked turkey, cut into ½-inch (1-cm) cubes (about 2 cups/500 mL) or meat picked off the carcass
½ cup (125 mL) wild rice (or brown rice)
Salt and pepper to taste
1 green onion, sliced
1 Tbsp (15 mL) chopped parsley

In a large pot, heat schmalz or oil on medium-high. Add onion, carrots, celery, and thyme, and sauté until the vegetables have softened, 3–4 minutes. Add stock, water, turkey, and wild rice, and bring to a boil. Reduce the heat to medium-low and simmer for 40 minutes to 1 hour, until the wild rice is cooked. (Alternatively, cook this in a pressure cooker on high for 30 minutes, then let the pressure naturally release.)

If you added fresh thyme sprigs, fish out and discard the stems, which should have donated their leaves to the soup. Adjust seasoning to taste with salt and pepper. Garnish with green onions and parsley and serve.

# Turkey & corn egg-drop soup

This comforting soup comes together in less than 10 minutes.

**Yield: 2–3 servings**

1 Tbsp (15 mL) turkey schmalz or other cooking oil
½ Tbsp (7.5 mL) grated fresh ginger
1 clove garlic, grated
1 19-oz (540-mL) can creamed corn
2 cups (500 mL) turkey or other stock, or water
5¼ oz (150 g) cooked turkey, cut into ½-inch (1-cm) cubes (about 1 cup/250 mL)
2 tsp (10 mL) soy sauce
1 egg, beaten
Salt and freshly ground black or white pepper to taste
1 tsp (5 mL) sesame oil
1 green onion, finely sliced on a bias

In a medium pot, heat schmalz or oil on medium-high. Add ginger and garlic and fry for 30 seconds until fragrant. Add creamed corn, stock or water, turkey, and soy sauce and bring to a boil.

While whisking or vigorously stirring the soup, gradually add the beaten egg in a thin stream.

Take the soup off the heat. Taste for seasoning and adjust as desired with salt and pepper. Stir in sesame oil, then portion soup into bowls. Garnish each bowl with green onions and serve.

# Turkey corn chowder

This hearty soup is a meal in itself—the kind of dish you'd imagine serving in a bread bowl, though I've yet to reach that level of plating ambition.

**Yield: 4–6 servings**

- 2 Tbsp (30 mL) turkey schmalz or other cooking oil
- 1 onion, diced
- 2 carrots, chopped
- 2 ribs celery, chopped
- 2 sprigs fresh thyme (or ½ tsp/2.5 mL dried thyme leaves)
- ⅓ cup (80 mL) all-purpose flour
- 4 cups (1 L) turkey or other stock
- 2 cups (500 mL) water
- 2 medium potatoes, diced (about 10½ oz/300 g)
- ½ tsp (2.5 mL) salt
- 10½ oz (300 g) cooked turkey, cut into 1-inch (2-cm) cubes (about 2½ cups/625 mL)
- 1 cup (250 mL) whipping cream
- 1 12-oz (341-mL) can corn, drained
- Salt and pepper to taste
- 1 Tbsp (15 mL) chopped parsley

Heat the schmalz or oil in a large pot on medium-high. Add onion, carrots, celery, and thyme and cook until the onion is soft and translucent, 3–5 minutes. Sprinkle in the flour and stir for 30 seconds, then gradually add the stock, stirring to break up any lumps of flour. Add the water, potatoes, and salt and turn the heat up to high.

Bring to a boil, then reduce the heat to medium and simmer until the potatoes are cooked, 12–15 minutes, stirring occasionally.

Stir in turkey, cream, and corn, and allow these to heat through, 2–3 minutes. Adjust seasoning to taste with salt and pepper, garnish with parsley, and serve.

# Turkey tom kha

Adapted from [Hot Thai Kitchen](). A game changer for me was learning from HTK's Pailin Chongchitnant that many of the aromatics—including lemongrass, galangal, makrut lime leaves, and Thai chilies—freeze incredibly well, so these days I always have some on hand. These frozen ingredients are much, much better than any dried alternatives. In the soup, they're meant to impart flavour and aroma but aren't meant to be eaten, so you could choose to remove them before serving.

**Yield: 4 servings**

- 2 cups (500 mL) turkey or other stock
- 1 14-oz (400-mL) can coconut milk
- 1 stalk lemongrass, bottom half only, smashed and cut into 2-inch (5-cm) pieces
- 12 thin slices galangal
- 5 makrut lime leaves, roughly torn into chunks
- 4 Thai chilies, cut in half on a bias
- 2 Tbsp (30 mL) fish sauce
- 1 Tbsp (15 mL) palm sugar or granulated sugar (½ oz/12 g)
- 1 lb (450 g) cooked turkey, cut into 1-inch (2-cm) cubes (about 3½ cups/875 mL)
- 7 oz (200 g) fresh mushrooms, in bite-sized pieces (I like a mix of shiitake, shimeji, and king oyster)
- 1½ Tbsp (22 mL) fresh lime juice
- ½ cup (125 mL) chopped cilantro

In a medium pot, combine stock, coconut milk, lemongrass, galangal, makrut lime leaves, and chilies, and bring to a boil on high heat. Reduce the heat to medium-low and simmer for 15 minutes.

Season with fish sauce and sugar, then add turkey and mushrooms. Simmer until turkey is heated through and mushrooms are cooked, 2–3 minutes.

Remove from the heat and stir in lime juice. Taste and adjust seasoning with more fish sauce, sugar, and lime juice as needed.

Portion soup into bowls, discarding the lemongrass, galangal, makrut lime leaves, and chilies.

Garnish each bowl with cilantro and serve.

# Turkey, sweet potato & peanut stew

This admittedly extremely westernized version of maafe is rich, filling, and endlessly adaptable: Use a scotch bonnet or habanero if you prefer more heat, or add a squeeze of lemon or splash of apple cider vinegar if you want a bit more tang. Wilt in more greens like kale or chard if you'd like to up the veg content. However you tweak it, it never disappoints.

**Yield: 4 servings**

1 Tbsp (15 mL) turkey schmalz or other cooking oil
1 onion, diced
3 cloves garlic, grated
1 Tbsp (15 mL) grated fresh ginger
1 jalapeño, small diced
2 tsp (10 mL) ground cumin
1 tsp (5 mL) ground coriander
1 tsp (5 mL) Kashmiri chili powder or paprika
½ tsp (2.5 mL) smoked paprika
3 cups (750 mL) turkey or other stock
1 14-oz (400-mL) can crushed tomatoes
1 sweet potato, peeled and cut into 1-inch (2-cm) cubes
½ tsp (2.5 mL) salt
¾ cup (180 mL) natural creamy peanut butter
10½ oz (300 g) cooked turkey, cut into 1-inch (2-cm) cubes (about 2½ cups/625 mL)
Salt and pepper to taste
4 oz (112 g) spinach, chopped into 1-inch (2-cm) segments
¼ cup (60 mL) unsalted roasted peanuts, chopped
1 green onion, sliced
2 Tbsp (30 mL) chopped cilantro
Rice or flatbreads, to serve

In a large pot, heat schmalz or oil on medium-high. Add onion and sauté for 3–4 minutes until translucent. Add garlic, ginger, jalapeño, cumin, coriander, chili powder or paprika, and smoked paprika. Sauté for 1 minute until the spices are fragrant.

Add stock, crushed tomatoes, sweet potatoes, and salt. Bring to a boil, then simmer until the sweet potatoes are fork-tender, 12–15 minutes.

Stir in peanut butter and turkey and allow them to heat through, 1–2 minutes. Taste and adjust seasoning with salt and pepper. Take the pot off the heat and stir in the spinach.

Garnish with chopped peanuts, green onions, and cilantro.

Serve with rice or flatbreads.

# Turkey quesadillas

These are eminently customizable—the only requirements, really, are the tortillas, cheese, and turkey. But what I'm sharing below is how I normally make them. I use large whole-grain tortillas, but use whatever you prefer!

**Yield: 4 quesadillas**

- 2 Tbsp (30 mL) turkey schmalz or other cooking oil
- 1 onion, diced
- 1 bell pepper (any colour), diced
- 4 cremini mushrooms, sliced
- 1 jalapeño, small diced
- 1 clove garlic, minced
- ½ tsp (2.5 mL) American-style chili powder
- ½ tsp (2.5 mL) ground cumin
- ½ tsp (2.5 mL) dried oregano
- ½ tsp (2.5 mL) smoked paprika
- 10½ oz (300 g) cooked turkey, shredded or cut into ½-inch (1-cm) cubes (about 2 cups/ 500 mL)
- 4 9½-inch (24-cm) flour tortillas
- 6 oz (170 g) shredded cheddar, Monterey Jack, or Oaxaca cheese (about 2 cups/ 500 mL)
- 8–12 pitted kalamata olives, sliced
- 2 green onions, sliced
- Greek yogurt or sour cream, to serve (optional)
- Pico de gallo or store-bought salsa, to serve (optional)
- Guacamole, to serve (optional)

In a large skillet, heat schmalz or oil on medium-high. Add onion, bell pepper, and mushrooms, and sauté for 3–4 minutes until vegetables are soft. Add jalapeño, garlic, chili powder, cumin, oregano, and smoked paprika and sauté 30 seconds or until fragrant. Add turkey meat and toss to coat it in the spices, then allow it to heat through, 1–2 minutes. Remove from the heat and set aside.

On a griddle or in a large skillet, heat a tortilla on medium-high. Sprinkle with a quarter of the cheese.

On one half of the tortilla, layer a quarter of the turkey mixture, a quarter of the olives, and a quarter of the green onions. Fold the other half overtop, then heat until one side is golden and crunchy, 2–3 minutes. Flip and let the other side to brown and crisp up, another 2–3 minutes, before removing to cool slightly on a wire rack while you finish making the rest of the quesadillas.

Repeat with the remaining tortillas, cheese, turkey mixture, olives, and green onions, until you've made 4 quesadillas.

Cut quesadillas into wedges and serve with yogurt or sour cream, pico de gallo or salsa, and guacamole, if desired.

# Sheet-pan turkey fajitas

This dish has one of the highest reward-to-effort ratios.

## Yield: 4 servings

2 tsp (10 mL) American-style chili powder
1 tsp (5 mL) ground cumin
1 tsp (5 mL) dried oregano
1 tsp (5 mL) garlic powder
1 tsp (5 mL) pepper
½ tsp (2.5 mL) smoked paprika
¼ tsp (1.2 mL) cayenne pepper
½ tsp (2.5 mL) salt
10½ oz (300 g) cooked turkey, torn into strips (about 2 cups/500 mL)
3 Tbsp (45 mL) turkey schmalz or other cooking oil, divided
Juice of ½ a lime
1 clove garlic, minced
1 green bell pepper, sliced
1 red bell pepper, sliced
1 yellow bell pepper, sliced
1 large onion, sliced
12 6-inch (15-cm) flour or corn tortillas
Salt and pepper to taste
2 Tbsp (30 mL) chopped cilantro
Greek yogurt or sour cream, to serve (optional)
Pico de gallo or store-bought tomato salsa, to serve (optional)
Guacamole, to serve (optional)
Jalapeño slices, fresh or pickled, to serve (optional)
Lime wedges, to serve

Make fajita seasoning by combining chili powder, cumin, oregano, garlic powder, pepper, smoked paprika, cayenne pepper, and salt in a small bowl.

In a medium bowl, toss the turkey meat with 1 Tbsp (15 mL) schmalz or oil, lime juice, garlic, and half of the fajita seasoning. Let this marinate for 20–30 minutes or up to overnight in the fridge.

Preheat the oven to 425°F (220°C).

To a large sheet pan, add bell peppers and onions. Drizzle over the remaining 2 Tbsp (30 mL) schmalz or oil, and add the remaining fajita seasoning. Toss until vegetables are evenly coated with the spices.

Roast 10–12 minutes, until the peppers begin to soften. Give the peppers and onions a stir, then add the turkey and bake another 4–6 minutes until the meat is heated through. If you prefer a bit of char, turn on the broiler for about 1 minute.

Meanwhile, put the tortillas in a lidded heatproof container, like a casserole dish.

Remove the sheet pan from the oven and turn the oven off, and put the container of tortillas in the oven to gently warm and soften in the residual heat for 5–10 minutes.

Taste the fajita mixture and adjust seasoning with salt and pepper as needed. Garnish with chopped cilantro.

Each person can assemble their own fajitas by filling warmed tortillas with the turkey and vegetables, topping with optional yogurt or sour cream, pico de gallo or salsa, guacamole, and jalapeño, and finishing with a squeeze of lime.

# Turkey enchiladas

This dish is a bit more involved, but it is incredibly forgiving and consistently delicious. Feel free to use store-bought enchilada sauce, but I've included a recipe here if you want to make your own.

**Yield: 4 servings**

## Enchilada sauce

- 1½ Tbsp (22 mL) turkey schmalz or other cooking oil
- 1 clove garlic, minced
- 2 Tbsp (30 mL) American-style chili powder
- 1 tsp (5 mL) ground cumin
- ½ tsp (2.5 mL) dried oregano
- 1½ Tbsp (22 mL) all-purpose flour
- 1 cup (250 mL) turkey or other stock
- 1 7.2-oz (213-mL) can tomato sauce
- 1 small chipotle pepper + ½ Tbsp (7.5 mL) adobo sauce
- ½ tsp (2.5 mL) salt

## Enchiladas

- 1 Tbsp (15 mL) turkey schmalz or other cooking oil
- 1 onion, diced
- 2 cloves garlic, minced
- 2 jalapeños, small diced
- 10½ oz (300 g) cooked turkey, shredded (about 2 cups/ 500 mL)
- 1 19-oz (540-mL) can black beans, rinsed and drained
- 1 12-oz (341-mL) can corn, drained

## Enchilada sauce

Heat schmalz or oil in a medium saucepan on medium heat. Add garlic and fry for 30 seconds until fragrant. Whisk in chili powder, cumin, oregano, and flour and fry for a few seconds to aromatize the spices. The mixture will look dry.

Slowly add the stock, whisking constantly to work out any lumps. Add tomato sauce and bring to a simmer. Continue heating the mixture, stirring occasionally, until it has thickened, 5–8 minutes. Remove from the heat and allow to cool for 10–20 minutes.

Add chipotle, adobo sauce, and salt, then blend smooth with an immersion blender. Refrigerate until needed.

## Enchiladas

In a large skillet, heat the schmalz or oil on medium-high. Add the onion and sauté until it starts to soften, about 3 minutes. Add garlic and jalapeños and sauté for 30 seconds. Transfer this mixture to a large mixing bowl. Add the cooked turkey, black beans, corn, 1 cup (250 mL) of the cheese, chili powder, cumin, oregano, salt, pepper, and ½ cup (125 mL) of enchilada sauce. Stir until well combined.

Preheat the oven to 350°F (180°C).

Heat each tortilla in a dry skillet on high heat for 15–20 seconds to soften it. Pile tortillas on a small plate and cover with a clean tea towel to keep them warm.

- 9 oz (255 g) shredded cheddar, Monterey Jack, Oaxaca cheese, or a mix (about 3 cups/750 mL), divided
- 1 tsp (5 mL) American-style chili powder
- 1 tsp (5 mL) ground cumin
- ½ tsp (2.5 mL) dried oregano
- ½ tsp (2.5 mL) salt
- ¼ tsp (1.2 mL) pepper
- 12 6-inch (15-cm) corn tortillas
- ½ cup (125 mL) chopped cilantro
- Greek yogurt or sour cream, to serve
- Lime wedges, to serve

Spread ½ cup (125 mL) of enchilada sauce over the bottom of a 9 × 13-inch (23 × 33-cm) baking dish.

To assemble an enchilada, place ½ cup (125 mL) of the turkey mixture down the middle of a tortilla and roll it up tightly.

Put the enchilada, seam side down, in the prepared baking dish. Repeat with remaining tortillas and turkey mixture.

Spread the remaining sauce (about 1½ cups/375 mL) over the enchiladas. Sprinkle on the remaining cheese.

Bake enchiladas for 20–25 minutes. Let rest for 5 minutes and then top with cilantro and serve with Greek yogurt or sour cream and wedges of lime.

# Turkey salad with cranberries & pecans

After a heavy meal, nothing is more refreshing than a zippy green salad packed with lean protein. White meat sliced thin tends to yield a more aesthetically pleasing result, but if you don't care about that, use whatever turkey leftovers you have on hand. The honey mustard vinaigrette calls for Dijon mustard for its emulsifying properties and grainy mustard for its little pops of texture, but use either one if you don't have both!

**Yield: 2 servings as a meal or 4 servings as a starter**

### Honey mustard vinaigrette

3 Tbsp (45 mL) lemon juice
¼ cup (60 mL) olive oil
1 tsp (5 mL) honey
1 tsp (5 mL) Dijon mustard
1 tsp (5 mL) grainy mustard
Salt and pepper to taste

### Salad

5¼ oz (150 g) lettuce, torn into bite-sized pieces
2½ oz (70 g) arugula
2½ oz (70 g) spinach
½ cucumber, halved lengthwise and sliced on a bias
1 carrot, peeled into ribbons
20 cherry tomatoes
¼ bell pepper (any colour), sliced
¼ red onion, sliced
⅓ cup (80 mL) dried cranberries
5¼ oz (150 g) sliced turkey (about 1 cup/250 mL)
⅓ cup (80 mL) pecans, slivered almonds, or pumpkin seeds
Crispy turkey skin, crumbled (optional)

### Honey mustard vinaigrette

Whisk together lemon juice, olive oil, honey, and mustards. Season to taste with salt and pepper. Alternatively, combine all ingredients in a small lidded jar and shake until mixed.

### Salad

In a large salad bowl, combine lettuce, arugula, spinach, cucumber, carrots, cherry tomatoes, bell pepper, onions, and cranberries. Pour over three-quarters of the dressing and toss to coat everything evenly. Portion the salad into individual bowls, then top each bowl with turkey, nuts, turkey skin (if using), and a drizzle of the dressing.

# Turkey cellophane noodle salad

This salad can be served chilled or at room temperature and offers a delightful variety of textures and fresh, herb-forward flavours.

**Yield: 4 servings**

### Dressing

1 red chili, thinly sliced
1 clove garlic, minced
1 tsp (5 mL) grated fresh ginger
3 Tbsp (45 mL) fresh lime juice
2 Tbsp (30 mL) fish sauce
1 Tbsp (15 mL) hoisin sauce
1 Tbsp (15 mL) sesame oil

### Salad

2½ oz (70 g) dried mung bean vermicelli noodles (2 bundles)
¼ oz (7 g) dried wood ear mushroom slivers, soaked for 2 hours (optional)
10½ oz (300 g) cooked turkey, shredded (about 2 cups/ 500 mL)
2 cups (500 mL) finely sliced cabbage (6¼ oz/180 g)
1 cucumber, cut in half lengthwise and sliced on a bias (about 8¾ oz/250 g)
1 carrot, julienned
2 green onions, finely sliced on a bias
¾ oz (20 g) cilantro leaves (about 1 lightly packed cup)
¾ oz (20 g) mint leaves (about 1 lightly packed cup)
½ cup (125 mL) unsalted roasted peanuts or cashews, roughly chopped, divided

### Dressing

In a small bowl, combine all the ingredients.

### Salad

Bring a small pot of water to a boil. Add noodles and wood ear mushroom slivers, if using, and cook until the noodles are soft, about 4 minutes. Drain in a sieve and rinse with cold water. Let the noodles and mushrooms drip dry in the sieve for a few minutes, then transfer them to a large mixing bowl. Add turkey, cabbage, cucumber, carrots, green onions, cilantro, mint, and about half of the nuts. Add dressing and toss to mix well. Top with the remaining nuts and serve.

# Turkey laab

This is a great way to use up the meat you pulled from the carcass after making stock because the dressing adds so much flavour, but feel free to use whatever leftover turkey you have. To turn this dish from an appetizer to a full meal, serve with sticky rice and cucumber slices. This recipe was adapted from Pailin Chongchitnant's "Leftover Anything Laab" recipe in her *Sabai* cookbook.

### Yield: 2 servings

1 Tbsp (15 mL) uncooked jasmine or Thai glutinous rice
1 makrut lime leaf (fresh or frozen)
5¼ oz (150 g) cooked turkey, shredded into ½-inch (1-cm) pieces or smaller (about 1 cup/250 mL), room temperature
1 Tbsp (15 mL) fish sauce
1 Tbsp (15 mL) fresh lime juice
¼ tsp (1.2 mL) granulated sugar
¼ tsp (1.2 mL) chili flakes
3 Tbsp (22 g) finely julienned shallots or red onion
1 green onion, sliced
¼ oz (7 g) mint leaves (about ¼ lightly packed cup/60 mL)
6–8 butter lettuce leaves
Cooked sticky rice, to serve (optional)
12–16 slices cucumber, to serve (optional)

Turn on your kitchen exhaust fan because this next step can get smoky. In a small skillet, toast rice and the lime leaf on high heat until the rice is a deep dark brown and the lime leaf has dried out and crisped up, 6–8 minutes. (If the lime leaf starts browning before the rice is ready, remove it and continue toasting the rice on its own.) Transfer the rice and lime leaf to a mortar (or spice grinder) and grind until you have a coarse powder.

In a large bowl, combine turkey, fish sauce, lime juice, sugar, chili flakes, shallots or red onion, green onions, mint, and the toasted rice powder. Toss to mix well and serve immediately with lettuce leaves (and, if desired, sticky rice and cucumber slices) so that each person can make their own lettuce wraps.

# Gochujang cashew turkey

Is there anything gochujang can't improve?

You can take this dish in any number of directions: Add some broccoli florets, green beans, or sugar snap peas to pack in more vegetables—or add diced pineapple for a sweet-and-sour vibe. This stir-fry is fantastic served on rice alongside a fried egg.

**Yield: 4 servings**

## Sauce

- 2 Tbsp (30 mL) gochujang
- 1 Tbsp (15 mL) soy sauce
- 2 tsp (10 mL) honey or granulated sugar
- ½ tsp (2.5 mL) sesame oil

## Stir-fry

- 2 Tbsp (30 mL) turkey schmalz or other cooking oil
- 1 onion, diced
- 1 Tbsp (15 mL) grated fresh ginger
- 3 cloves garlic, minced
- ½ green bell pepper, diced
- 1 red bell pepper, diced
- 10½ oz (300 g) cooked turkey, cut into ½-inch (1-cm) cubes (about 2 cups/500 mL)
- ½ cup (125 mL) cashews, roasted
- 1 green onion, sliced
- 2 tsp (10 mL) sesame seeds, toasted

## Sauce

In a small bowl, combine all the sauce ingredients and stir to dissolve the honey or sugar.

## Stir-fry

To a wok or skillet on medium-high, add schmalz or oil, followed by the onion. Sauté until onion is translucent, 2–3 minutes, then add ginger and garlic and cook until fragrant, about 1 minute. Add peppers, turkey, cashews, and the sauce. Stir-fry until the sauce thickens into a glaze and coats everything evenly, about 3 minutes. Remove from the heat. (This amount of cooking leaves the peppers with a fresh bite. If you prefer your peppers to be more tender, add them on their own and stir-fry for 2 minutes or so before adding the turkey and cashews.)

Garnish with green onions and sesame seeds and serve.

# Saag turkey

This dish is a vibrant, delicious way to use up some of the leafy greens that might have lingered in your crisper drawer for a while, including sometimes-awkward-to-use ingredients like radish or turnip tops. Feel free to add paneer if you want to play a fun game of white-cube-of-protein roulette.

**Yield: 4 servings**

10½ oz (300 g) cooked turkey, cut into 1-inch (2-cm) cubes (about 2½ cups/625 mL)
1 Tbsp + 1 tsp (20 mL) turkey schmalz or other cooking oil, divided
1 Tbsp (15 mL) garam masala, divided
1 tsp (5 mL) cumin seeds
1 onion, diced
1 jalapeño, small diced
1 Tbsp (15 mL) grated fresh ginger
1 Tbsp (15 mL) grated garlic (3–4 cloves)
1½ Tbsp (22 mL) ground coriander
½ tsp (2.5 mL) ground turmeric
½ tsp (2.5 mL) Kashmiri chili powder or paprika
1 tsp (5 mL) salt
½ cup (125 mL) water
8 oz (225 g) spinach, chopped into 1-inch (2-cm) segments
4 oz (112 g) greens, like mustard greens, radish tops, turnip tops, chard, beet greens, or more spinach, chopped into 1-inch (2-cm) segments
Juice of ½ a lime
Salt and pepper to taste
2 Tbsp (30 mL) whipping cream or plain yogurt
Rice or naan, to serve

In a medium bowl, toss the turkey cubes with 1 tsp (5 mL) of the schmalz or oil and 1 tsp (5 mL) of the garam masala. Set aside.

In a medium pot on medium-high heat, add the remaining 1 Tbsp (15 mL) schmalz or oil and the cumin seeds, and cook until the cumin seeds sizzle, about 3 minutes. Add onion, jalapeño, ginger, and garlic, reduce the heat to medium and sauté until the ingredients are deeply caramelized, 7–8 minutes. If the ingredients look as though they're on the verge of burning, turn down the heat or add a splash of water.

Add the remaining 2 tsp (10 mL) garam masala, coriander, turmeric, chili powder or paprika, and salt, and cook for 1 minute, then deglaze with ½ cup (125 mL) water. Add the spinach and greens, and stir until just wilted, about 2 minutes.

Remove from the heat. Using a blender or an immersion blender, purée the spinach mixture till smooth. If the mixture is too thick for your liking, stir in a splash of water to thin it out.

Return the pot to medium-high heat and add turkey. Simmer for about 5 minutes until the turkey is heated through. Take it off the heat, and add lime juice. Taste and adjust seasoning with salt and pepper.

Transfer to a serving dish and garnish with a drizzle of cream or a dollop of yogurt.

Serve with rice or naan.

# Turkey curry rice

If you have Japanese curry roux cubes, by all means use those to make your sauce. I don't usually have them on hand, so this recipe involves making a simple roux from scratch, adapted from [Just One Cookbook](). 

**Yield: 4 servings**

### Curry roux

4 oz (112 g) butter
1½ Tbsp (22.5 mL) grated fresh ginger
¼ cup (60 mL) curry powder
1 Tbsp (15 mL) garam masala
½ cup (125 mL) all-purpose flour

### Curry

2 Tbsp (30 mL) turkey schmalz or other cooking oil
1 onion, cut into 1-inch (2-cm) chunks
1 clove garlic, minced
8 oz (225 g) carrots (about 2 large or 3 medium), cut into 1-inch (2-cm) chunks, or baby carrots
1 lb (450 g) potatoes, peeled and cut into 1-inch (2-cm) cubes
1 apple, peeled and grated
1 Tbsp (15 mL) soy sauce
1 Tbsp (15 mL) honey
1 Tbsp (15 mL) tomato paste
4 cups (1 L) turkey or other stock
13 oz (370 g) cooked turkey, cut into 1-inch (2-cm) cubes (about 3 cups/750 mL)
Salt and pepper to taste
Rice, to serve

### Curry roux

In a small saucepan, heat butter on medium until it has melted and started to brown, about 5 minutes. Add ginger, curry powder, and garam masala and fry for 30 seconds to aromatize the spices. Reduce the heat to low and whisk in the flour, then cook, stirring frequently, for 5 minutes. The mixture will look dry. Remove from the heat and set aside.

### Curry

In a large pot, heat schmalz or oil on medium. Add onion and garlic and cook until browned, about 8 minutes. Raise heat to high, then add carrots, potatoes, apple, soy sauce, honey, tomato paste, and stock. Bring to a boil, then simmer until the potatoes are tender, 12–15 minutes. Stir in curry roux until it is evenly distributed, then stir in the turkey and cook 2–5 minutes or until the curry is thickened to your liking. Adjust seasoning to taste with salt and pepper. Serve with rice.

# Hainanese turkey rice

This dish is certainly not going to have the depth of flavour that you'd get from authentic, labour-intensive Hainanese chicken rice, but if the point is to use up leftover turkey in a quick and tasty way, this is a decent tribute to the real thing. This recipe flavours the turkey with a ginger-green onion topping, but many Singaporean-style Hainanese chicken rice recipes might suggest using a chili garlic sauce. Use what you prefer!

**Yield: 2 servings**

### Ginger-green onion topping

2 Tbsp (30 mL) grated fresh ginger
2 green onions, finely sliced
1 clove garlic, grated
½ tsp (2.5 mL) salt
¼ tsp (1.2 mL) chili flakes (optional)
¼ cup (60 mL) neutral oil

### Rice

1 cup (250 mL) uncooked white rice
2 Tbsp (30 mL) turkey schmalz or other cooking oil
2 cloves garlic, minced
2 tsp (10 mL) grated fresh ginger
1¾ cups (430 mL) turkey or other stock

### Ginger-green onion topping

Combine ginger, green onions, garlic, salt, and chili flakes (if using) in a small heatproof bowl. In a small skillet or saucepan, heat the oil on high until it shimmers and verges on smoking. Carefully pour the hot oil over the ginger mixture—it will sizzle and fill the air with a gingery aroma. Let the mixture cool to room temperature.

### Rice

Put rice in a sieve and rinse it until the water runs clear. Let the rice drip dry for 5 minutes in the sieve, and shake the sieve in long tossing motions to try to get out as much water as possible. The drier you get the rice at this stage, the less time the next step will take.

In a medium pot, heat the schmalz or oil on high. Add garlic and ginger and fry until fragrant, 1–2 minutes. Add the rice and stir to coat all the grains with schmalz. Continue heating the rice until no moisture remains, 2–4 minutes.

If you're using a rice cooker: Transfer the rice mixture to the rice cooker, add the stock, then activate the rice cooker. (I use all 1¾ cups (430 mL) of stock called for, but I have an older, simpler rice cooker. Newer rice cookers are more efficient at trapping in steam, so if you use one, you might need to experiment with a smaller amount of stock. Start with 1¼ cups (310 mL) and see if you have to adjust for next time!)

### To serve

1 lb (450 g) cooked turkey, cut into 1-inch (2-cm) slices
½ cucumber, sliced (about 4½ oz/125 g)

If you're cooking the rice on the stove: Add the stock, bring the mixture to a boil, then lower the heat to medium-low and simmer, covered, for 12–15 minutes, or until the rice has absorbed the liquid. Remove the pot from the heat and let it stand, covered, for 10 minutes.

### To serve

Divide the rice between two plates or bowls. Top each portion with half the turkey and half the cucumber slices. Spoon the ginger–green onion topping over each portion of turkey and serve.

# Turkey fried rice

Fried rice is the quintessential fridge-clearing meal, and the turkey's just playing a supporting role here. Use whatever you have on hand, of course, but this is a great way to use broccoli stems if you're using only the florets in other dishes. Just peel off the tough outer layer and dice.

What's made the biggest difference in my fried rice is finally getting a bottle of dark soy sauce. I used to use light soy sauce alone because I didn't want to store another bottle of sauce, but I've found that as much as Chinese cooks sing the praises of *wok hay*, the dark soy and Shaoxing wine are what give my fried rice 80% of that distinctive, moreish Chinese takeout flavour.

**Yield: 4 servings**

2 Tbsp (30 mL) turkey schmalz or other cooking oil, divided
2 eggs, beaten
1 Tbsp (15 mL) grated fresh ginger
1 clove garlic, minced
1 onion, diced
4–6 cremini or shiitake mushrooms, diced
2 broccoli stems, peeled and diced
5¼ oz (150 g) cooked turkey, cut into ½-inch (1-cm) cubes (about 1 cup/250 mL)
4 cups (1 L) cooked rice (day-old is best)
2 tsp (10 mL) light soy sauce, plus more if needed
1 tsp (5 mL) dark soy sauce
1 tsp (5 mL) Shaoxing wine
½ tsp (2.5 mL) sesame oil
1 green onion, sliced
Freshly ground black or white pepper

Heat a wok or large skillet on medium-high and add 1 Tbsp (15 mL) schmalz or oil. When the schmalz is fluid and shimmers, add eggs and scramble until cooked, 2–3 minutes. Remove from the wok and roughly chop the egg into ½-inch (1-cm) pieces.

Add the remaining 1 Tbsp (15 mL) schmalz or oil to the wok. Add ginger, garlic, and onion, and stir-fry until the onion is soft, 2–3 minutes. Add mushrooms and broccoli stems, sautéing until mushrooms are cooked and broccoli stems are tender-crisp. Add turkey, rice, and egg, and stir to break up any lumps of rice. Add soy sauces and Shaoxing wine, and stir-fry for about 5 minutes or until the rice starts to get crispy and smell fragrant.

Remove from the heat, add sesame oil and green onions, and toss to mix, then season to taste with more light soy sauce and pepper before serving.

# Turkey okonomiyaki

This recipe is not at all authentic—there's no mountain yam, no bonito flakes, no dashi—but it's easy and filling. Feel free to add other proteins for a variety of flavours; squid, diced shrimp, and ground pork have all worked well for me.

**Yield: 3 pancakes**

### Okonomiyaki sauce

2 Tbsp (30 mL) ketchup
1 Tbsp (15 mL) Worcestershire sauce
1 Tbsp (15 mL) soy sauce
1 tsp (5 mL) honey or granulated sugar

### Okonomiyaki batter

3 cups (750 mL) shredded cabbage
3 eggs
1 cup (250 mL) all-purpose flour
2 Tbsp (30 mL) cornstarch
1 tsp (5 mL) salt
¼ tsp (1.2 mL) pepper
1 cup (250 mL) turkey or other stock, or water
1 tsp (5 mL) chopped pickled ginger
2 green onions, sliced
5¼ oz (150 g) cooked turkey, shredded or cut into ½-inch (1-cm) cubes (about 1 cup/ 250 mL)

### Okonomiyaki sauce

In a small bowl, stir together all the sauce ingredients until the honey or sugar is dissolved.

### Okonomiyaki batter

Mix all ingredients well and set aside for 20 minutes to hydrate the flour. ☞☞☞

## To serve

4½ Tbsp (70 mL) turkey schmalz or other cooking oil, divided
Kewpie mayo
2 tsp (10 mL) sesame seeds, toasted
1 green onion, sliced
Pickled ginger

## To serve

In a large skillet, heat 1½ Tbsp (22 mL) schmalz or oil on medium-high, then add about a third of the batter, spreading it to about ½ inch (1 cm) thick. Fry until golden brown on one side, 3–4 minutes, then flip and fry until golden brown on the other side, about 2 minutes, adding oil if necessary.

Repeat until all the batter is cooked.

Top each pancake with Kewpie mayo, okonomiyaki sauce, toasted sesame seeds, green onions, and pickled ginger.

# Turkey kookoo

These little Persian-inspired patties make a great snack or a light lunch when paired with a fresh salad. Many traditional recipes call for saffron, but I don't usually bother, relying instead on the turmeric to give the patties their golden hue. If your mashed potatoes are on the loose side, you might need to add some potato starch or cornstarch to absorb some of the moisture so that you can form patties that will hold their shape. Alternatively, cook the whole mixture together like a frittata and cut into wedges to serve. I eat these with just a dollop of Greek yogurt, but they'd also be delicious with a garlicky sauce like tzatziki, aioli, or toum.

**Yield: 10 patties**

1 large onion, grated
1½ cups (375 mL) leftover mashed potatoes or 12 oz (340 g) potatoes, boiled until soft and mashed
7 oz (200 g) cooked turkey, shredded (about 1⅓ cups/ 330 mL)
2 cloves garlic, grated
¼ cup (60 mL) chopped parsley
1 tsp (5 mL) ground turmeric
½ tsp (2.5 mL) salt
½ tsp (2.5 mL) pepper
1 egg
Potato starch or cornstarch, as needed
¼ cup (60 mL) turkey schmalz or other cooking oil, divided
2 Tbsp (30 mL) Greek yogurt, to serve

With the help of a fine-mesh sieve or clean tea towel, squeeze most of the moisture out of the grated onion.

In a large mixing bowl, combine onion, potatoes, turkey, garlic, parsley, turmeric, salt, and pepper. Taste and adjust seasoning as needed.

Add egg and mix well. If the mixture is too loose for you to handle and form patties, add potato starch or cornstarch 1 Tbsp (15 mL) at a time until the mixture holds together.

Chill the mixture in the fridge for 10–15 minutes so that it becomes easier to handle.

Divide the mixture into 10 portions and shape one of the portions into a patty about ½ inch (1 cm) thick. Place it on a parchment-lined sheet pan and repeat until you've used up the potato-turkey mixture.

In a skillet, heat 1 Tbsp (15 mL) schmalz or oil on medium-high. Add as many patties will fit without overcrowding the skillet and fry until golden brown, 3–4 minutes. Flip and fry the other side until golden brown, 3–4 minutes.

Continue frying patties in batches, adding more schmalz or oil before each batch as needed, until all patties have been fried.

Serve with Greek yogurt or another sauce you like.

# Turkey croquettes

These are similar to the turkey kookoo (page 54), but they involve the further step of breading the patties with panko before frying. It's fine if your mashed potatoes have already been flavoured with yogurt, sour cream, or herbs or if you want to sub some of the potato with mashed sweet potato or pumpkin purée—our aim is deliciousness, not authenticity. Speaking of which, Japanese-style croquettes are usually deep-fried, but I generally can't be arsed to heat up that much oil, so I shallow-fry. Air-frying also works.

If you have particularly loose mashed potatoes, you might have to add some potato starch or cornstarch to absorb some of the excess moisture until you can easily handle the patty mixture. And if you, like me, hate wasting the unused breading ingredients—the flour, egg, and panko—you can throw them into the batter for okonomiyaki (page 52).

**Yield: 8 croquettes**

½ Tbsp (7.5 mL) turkey schmalz or other cooking oil
1 shallot (or small onion), finely diced
1 medium carrot, finely diced
1 clove garlic, minced
4¼ oz (120 g) cooked turkey, finely diced (about ¾ cup/ 180 mL)
1 tsp (5 mL) Worcestershire sauce or soy sauce or 1 Tbsp (15 mL) leftover gravy
2 cups (500 mL) leftover mashed potatoes or 1 lb (450 g) potatoes, boiled until soft and mashed
Salt and pepper to taste
Potato starch or cornstarch, as needed

Heat schmalz or oil in a skillet on medium-high heat. Add shallot and carrot and sauté until the shallot is translucent, about 3 minutes. Add the garlic and cook another 30 seconds, until fragrant. Add turkey and Worcestershire or soy sauce. Stir to evenly mix, then remove from the heat.

In a large mixing bowl, combine this mixture with the mashed potatoes. Taste for seasoning and adjust as desired with salt and pepper.

Divide the potato mixture into 8 portions, and shape each portion into a patty about ½ inch (1 cm) thick. (If the mixture is too loose to form patties, add 1 Tbsp (15 mL) potato starch or cornstarch and try again. Keep adding starch gradually until the mixture is dry enough to handle.) Place the patties on a parchment-lined sheet pan and put the sheet pan into the freezer for 10 minutes to allow the patties to firm up a bit.

3 Tbsp (45 mL) all-purpose flour
1 egg
¾ cup (180 mL) panko breadcrumbs
Neutral oil for frying
Kewpie mayo, to serve (optional)
Okonomiyaki sauce (page 52), to serve (optional)

Meanwhile, prepare your breading station: Place the flour in one shallow dish, gently beat the egg in a second shallow dish, and add panko to a third shallow dish.

Take the patties out of the freezer. Put one potato patty into the flour, coating all sides evenly and shaking off the excess, then the egg, then the panko. Press panko into the patties to ensure thorough coverage. Repeat with all of the patties.

If shallow frying: Add about 1 inch (2 cm) of frying oil to a skillet. Heat oil until it reaches 350°F (180°C). Fry patties in batches until crispy and golden brown, about 2 minutes on each side, and place them on a wire rack or paper towel-lined plate to drain.

If air-frying: Brush or spray patties with a thin coat of oil. Add as many patties as will fit without overcrowding the basket of an air-fryer preheated to 375°F (190°C) and cook for 8 minutes, flipping them halfway through. Repeat with the remaining patties until they have all been fried.

Serve the croquettes with Kewpie mayo and okonomiyaki sauce, if desired.

# Index

**A**

apple
  cranberry chutney, 13
  turkey curry rice, 46
arugula
  turkey cranberry sandwich, 12
  turkey salad with cranberries & pecans, 36

**B**

bánh mì, turkey, 14-15
beans, black, in turkey enchiladas, 34-35
beans, green
  breakfast hash, 10-11
  turkey cottage pie, 18-19
  turkey pie, 16-17
bell pepper
  gochujang cashew turkey, 42
  sheet-pan turkey fajitas, 32
  turkey quesadillas, 30
  turkey salad with cranberries & pecans, 36
black beans, in turkey enchiladas, 34-35
bread
  turkey cranberry sandwich, 12
  Vietnamese baguette, for turkey bánh mì, 14-15
breakfast hash, 10-11
brie, in turkey cranberry sandwich, 12
broccoli stems, in turkey fried rice, 50

**C**

cabbage
  turkey cellophane noodle salad, 38
  turkey okonomiyaki, 52-53
cardamom
  cranberry chutney, 13
  cranberry yogurt, 13
carrots
  pickled vegetables, 14
  turkey cellophane noodle salad, 38
  turkey corn chowder, 24
  turkey cottage pie, 18-19
  turkey croquettes, 56-57
  turkey curry rice, 46
  turkey pie, 16-17
  turkey salad with cranberries & pecans, 36
  turkey stock, 2
  turkey wild rice soup, 20
cashews
  gochujang cashew turkey, 42
  turkey cellophane noodle salad, 38
cayenne pepper, in sheet-pan turkey fajitas, 32
celery
  turkey corn chowder, 24
  turkey cottage pie, 18-19
  turkey pie, 16-17
  turkey stock, 2
  turkey wild rice soup, 20
cheddar
  breakfast hash, 10-11
  turkey cottage pie, 18-19
  turkey enchiladas, 34-35
  turkey quesadillas, 30
cheese. *See also* cheddar; Monterey Jack; Oaxaca cheese; parmesan
  brie, in turkey cranberry sandwich, 12
  breakfast hash, 10-11
cream cheese, in cranberry cheesecake, 13
  vegetable crackers, 4
cheesecake, cranberry, 13
chilies, fresh. *See also* jalapeño
  turkey cellophane noodle salad, 38
  turkey tom kha, 26
chili flakes
  cranberry chutney, 13
  ginger-green onion topping, 48
  turkey cottage pie, 18-19
  turkey laab, 40
chili powder
  enchilada sauce, 34
  sheet-pan turkey fajitas, 32
  turkey enchiladas, 34-35
  turkey quesadillas, 30
chipotle pepper, in enchilada sauce, 34
chowder, turkey corn, 24
chutney, cranberry, 13
cilantro
  sheet-pan turkey fajitas, 32
  turkey, sweet potato & peanut stew, 28
  turkey bánh mì, 14-15
  turkey cellophane noodle salad, 38
  turkey enchiladas, 34-35
  turkey tom kha, 26
cinnamon
  cranberry chutney, 13
  cranberry yogurt, 13
cloves, in cranberry chutney, 13
coconut milk, in turkey tom kha, 26
coriander. *See also* cilantro
  saag turkey, 44
  turkey, sweet potato & peanut stew, 28

corn
    turkey & corn egg-drop soup, 22
    turkey corn chowder, 24
    turkey cottage pie, 18–19
    turkey enchiladas, 34–35
    turkey pie, 16–17
cottage pie, turkey, 18–19
crackers, vegetable, 4
cranberries
    cranberry sauce, ideas for leftover, 13
    dried, in turkey salad with cranberries & pecans, 36
    turkey cranberry sandwich, 12
cream cheese, in cranberry cheesecake, 13
crispy turkey skin, 6
croquettes, turkey, 56–57
cucumber
    Hainanese turkey rice, 48–49
    turkey bánh mì, 14–15
    turkey cellophane noodle salad, 38
    turkey laab, 40
    turkey salad with cranberries & pecans, 36
cumin
    breakfast hash, 10–11
    enchilada sauce, 34
    saag turkey, 44
    sheet-pan turkey fajitas, 32
    turkey, sweet potato & peanut stew, 28
    turkey enchiladas, 34–35
    turkey quesadillas, 30
curry
    curry roux, 46
    saag turkey, 44
    turkey curry rice, 46

**D**
daikon radish, in pickled vegetables, 14
dressings. See sauces & dressings
dried fruit, in cranberry chutney, 13

**E**
eggs
    breakfast hash, 10–11
    turkey & corn egg-drop soup, 22
    turkey fried rice, 50
    turkey okonomiyaki, 52–53
enchiladas, turkey, 34–35
enchilada sauce, 34

**F**
fajitas, sheet-pan turkey, 32
fried rice, turkey, 50

**G**
galangal, in turkey tom kha, 26
garam masala
    saag turkey, 44
    turkey curry rice, 46
ginger
    ginger-green onion topping, 48
    gochujang cashew turkey, 42
    ground, in cranberry chutney, 13
    Hainanese turkey rice, 48–49
    pickled, in turkey okonomiyaki, 52–53
    saag turkey, 44
    turkey, sweet potato & peanut stew, 28
    turkey & corn egg-drop soup, 22
    turkey cellophane noodle salad, 38
    turkey curry rice, 46
    turkey fried rice, 50

gochujang cashew turkey, 42
green beans
    breakfast hash, 10–11
    turkey cottage pie, 18–19
    turkey pie, 16–17
green onions
    ginger-green onion topping, 48
    gochujang cashew turkey, 42
    turkey, sweet potato & peanut stew, 28
    turkey & corn egg-drop soup, 22
    turkey cellophane noodle salad, 38
    turkey fried rice, 50
    turkey laab, 40
    turkey okonomiyaki, 52–53
    turkey quesadillas, 30
    turkey wild rice soup, 20
greens. See also specific greens
    saag turkey, 44
    turkey salad with cranberries & pecans, 36

**H**
Hainanese turkey rice, 48–49
hash, breakfast, 10–11
hoisin sauce
    turkey bánh mì, 14–15
    turkey cellophane noodle salad, 38
honey
    cranberry yogurt, 13
    gochujang cashew turkey, 42
    honey mustard vinaigrette, 36
    okonomiyaki sauce, 52
    turkey curry rice, 46

**J**
jalapeño
    breakfast hash, 10–11
    saag turkey, 44

jalapeño *(cont'd)*
    turkey, sweet potato & peanut stew, 28
    turkey bánh mì, 14–15
    turkey enchiladas, 34–35
    turkey quesadillas, 30
Japanese curry, or turkey curry rice, 46

## K

Kashmiri chili powder
    saag turkey, 44
    turkey, sweet potato & peanut stew, 28
Kewpie mayo
    turkey bánh mì, 14–15
    turkey croquettes, 56–57
    turkey okonomiyaki, 52–53
kookoo, turkey, 54

## L

laab, turkey, 40
lemon, in honey mustard vinaigrette, 36
lemongrass, in turkey tom kha, 26
lettuce
    turkey laab, 40
    turkey salad with cranberries & pecans, 36
lime
    saag turkey, 44
    sheet-pan turkey fajitas, 32
    turkey bánh mì, 14–15
    turkey cellophane noodle salad, 38
    turkey enchiladas, 34–35
    turkey laab, 40
    turkey tom kha, 26
lime leaves, makrut
    turkey laab, 40
    turkey tom kha, 26

## M

maafe, or turkey, sweet potato & peanut stew, 28
makrut lime leaves
    turkey laab, 40
    turkey tom kha, 26
mashed potatoes
    turkey cottage pie, 18–19
    turkey croquettes, 56–57
    turkey kookoo, 54
mayo. *See* Kewpie mayo
mint
    turkey cellophane noodle salad, 38
    turkey laab, 40
miso paste, in turkey cottage pie, 18–19
mizuna, in turkey cranberry sandwich, 12
Monterey Jack
    turkey enchiladas, 34–35
    turkey quesadillas, 30
mung bean noodles, in turkey cellophane noodle salad, 38
mushrooms
    cremini, in turkey quesadillas, 30
    cremini or shiitake, in turkey fried rice, 50
    turkey tom kha, 26
    wood ear, in turkey cellophane noodle salad, 38
mustard honey vinaigrette, 36

## N

noodles, in turkey cellophane noodle salad, 38

## O

Oaxaca cheese
    turkey enchiladas, 34–35
    turkey quesadillas, 30
okonomiyaki, turkey, 52–53
okonomiyaki sauce, 52
olives, in turkey quesadillas, 30
onions
    pickled vegetables, 14
    sheet-pan turkey fajitas, 32
    turkey cranberry sandwich, 12
    turkey curry rice, 46
    turkey laab, 40
    turkey salad with cranberries & pecans, 36
orange
    cranberry cheesecake, 13
    cranberry chutney, 13
oregano
    breakfast hash, 10–11
    enchilada sauce, 34
    sheet-pan turkey fajitas, 32
    turkey enchiladas, 34–35
    turkey quesadillas, 30

## P

panko breadcrumbs, in turkey croquettes, 56–57
paprika. *See also* smoked paprika
    saag turkey, 44
    turkey, sweet potato & peanut stew, 28
parmesan
    turkey cottage pie, 18–19
    vegetable crackers, 4
parsley
    turkey corn chowder, 24
    turkey kookoo, 54
    turkey wild rice soup, 20
peanuts
    turkey, sweet potato & peanut stew, 28
    turkey cellophane noodle salad, 38
pear, in cranberry chutney, 13

peas, snap
    turkey cottage pie, 18–19
    turkey pie, 16–17
pecans & cranberries, turkey salad with, 36
pickled ginger, in turkey okonomiyaki, 52–53
pickled vegetables, 14
pie
    turkey cottage pie, 18–19
    turkey pie, 16–17
potatoes
    breakfast hash, 10–11
    mashed, in turkey cottage pie, 18–19
    mashed, in turkey croquettes, 56–57
    mashed, in turkey kookoo, 54
    turkey corn chowder, 24
    turkey curry rice, 46
    turkey pie, 16–17

## Q
quesadillas, turkey, 30

## R
red onions
    turkey cranberry sandwich, 12
    turkey laab, 40
    turkey salad with cranberries & pecans, 36
rice
    Hainanese turkey rice, 48–49
    turkey curry rice, 46
    turkey fried rice, 50
    turkey laab, 40
rosemary
    turkey cottage pie, 18–19
    turkey pie, 16–17
    vegetable crackers, 4
rutabaga, in turkey pie, 16–17

## S
saag turkey, 44
sage
    turkey pie, 16–17
    vegetable crackers, 4
salad
    turkey cellophane noodle salad, 38
    turkey laab, 40
    turkey salad with cranberries & pecans, 36
sandwiches
    turkey bánh mì, 14–15
    turkey cranberry, 12
sauces & dressings
    curry roux, 46
    dressing, for turkey cellophane noodle salad, 38
    enchilada sauce, 34
    ginger–green onion topping, 48
    for gochujang cashew turkey, 42
    honey mustard vinaigrette, 36
    okonomiyaki sauce, 52
schmalz, turkey, 6
sesame oil
    gochujang cashew turkey, 42
    turkey & corn egg-drop soup, 22
    turkey cellophane noodle salad, 38
    turkey fried rice, 50
sesame seeds
    gochujang cashew turkey, 42
    turkey okonomiyaki, 52–53
shallots
    turkey croquettes, 56–57
    turkey laab, 40
Shaoxing wine, in turkey fried rice, 50
sheet-pan turkey fajitas, 32
shiitake mushrooms, in turkey fried rice, 50
skin, crispy, 6
smoked paprika
    breakfast hash, 10–11
    sheet-pan turkey fajitas, 32
    turkey, sweet potato & peanut stew, 28
    turkey quesadillas, 30
snap peas
    turkey cottage pie, 18–19
    turkey pie, 16–17
soup
    turkey & corn egg-drop soup, 22
    turkey corn chowder, 24
    turkey tom kha, 26
    turkey wild rice soup, 20
sour cream, for turkey enchiladas, 34–35
soy sauce
    gochujang cashew turkey, 42
    okonomiyaki sauce, 52
    turkey & corn egg-drop soup, 22
    turkey croquettes, 56–57
    turkey curry rice, 46
    turkey fried rice, 50
spinach
    saag turkey, 44
    turkey, sweet potato & peanut stew, 28
    turkey salad with cranberries & pecans, 36
stew, turkey, sweet potato & peanut, 28
stock, turkey, 2
sweet potatoes
    breakfast hash, 10–11
    turkey, sweet potato & peanut stew, 28

## T

Thai chilies, in turkey tom kha, 26
thyme
- turkey corn chowder, 24
- turkey cottage pie, 18–19
- turkey pie, 16–17
- turkey stock, 2
- turkey wild rice soup, 20

tomatoes
- turkey, sweet potato & peanut stew, 28
- turkey salad with cranberries & pecans, 36

tomato paste
- turkey cottage pie, 18–19
- turkey curry rice, 46

tomato sauce, in enchilada sauce, 34
tom kha, turkey, 26
tortillas
- sheet-pan turkey fajitas, 32
- turkey enchiladas, 34–35
- turkey quesadillas, 30

turmeric
- saag turkey, 44
- turkey kookoo, 54

## V

vegetables, leftover. *See also specific vegetables*
- breakfast hash, 10–11
- turkey cottage pie, 18–19
- turkey pie, 16–17
- vegetable crackers, 4

Vietnamese baguette, for turkey bánh mì, 14–15

## W

wild rice soup, turkey, 20
wood ear mushroom, in turkey cellophane noodle salad, 38
Worcestershire sauce
- okonomiyaki sauce, 52
- turkey cottage pie, 18–19
- turkey croquettes, 56–57

## Y

yogurt
- cranberry yogurt, 13
- saag turkey, 44
- sheet-pan turkey fajitas, 32
- turkey enchiladas, 34–35
- turkey kookoo, 54
- turkey quesadillas, 30

## Links to recipes referenced

**Page 4**: Min Kwon, "Easy Sweet Potato Crackers," MJ & Hungryman, mjandhungryman.com/sweet-potato-crackers/

**Page 26**: Pailin Chongchitnant, "Authentic Tom Kha Gai (Thai Coconut Chicken Soup)," Hot Thai Kitchen, hot-thai-kitchen.com/tom-ka-gai/

**Page 46**: Namiko Hirasawa Chen, "How to Make Japanese Curry Roux," Just One Cookbook, justonecookbook.com/how-to-make-curry-roux/